To Build a Fire

*A Brutal Tale of Survival, Instinct &
Man's Battle Against Nature's Frozen
Wrath*

A Modern Translation
Adapted for the Contemporary Reader

Jack London

Translated by Tim Zengerink

Table of Contents

Preface
Message to the Reader

Rebuilding the Greatest Library in Human History

Thousands of years ago, the Library of Alexandria was the heart of global knowledge — a sanctuary where the wisdom of every known civilization was gathered and shared freely.

And then, it was lost.

Now, we're rebuilding it — and you are invited to join us.

At the Library of Alexandria, we've set out to make every book available to every person on Earth — not just in print, but in every language, every format, and for every reader.

Here's how we do it:

- **Deluxe Print Editions at True Printing Cost** - Order any book as a high-quality paperback, elegant hardcover, or stunning boxset — and only pay what it costs to print. No markups. No middlemen.
- **Unlimited Access to the Greatest Works** - Enjoy thousands of timeless classics — from Plato to Shakespeare to Tolstoy — in beautiful, modern eBook and audiobook editions. Read and listen without limits — for every reader, everywhere.
- **Modern Translations for Every Language & Dialect** - We're reimagining the classics in clear, accessible language — and translating them into every dialect imaginable. Everyone deserves to understand humanity's greatest ideas.

When you visit **LibraryofAlexandria.com**, you're not just accessing books — you're joining a global movement to restore, preserve, and share the wisdom of civilization.

Join us today at LibraryofAlexandria.com

Together, we'll ensure the light of human wisdom never fades again.

With gratitude,

The Modern Library of Alexandria Team

Visit:
www.libraryofalexandria.com
Or scan the code below:

Introduction

The Stark Reality of Survival

Jack London's *To Build a Fire* is one of the most enduring short stories in American literature, a tale that captures the raw struggle of man against the merciless forces of nature. First published in 1902 (and later revised in 1908 into its more famous form), this story embodies the essence of naturalism—an unflinching depiction of human vulnerability, fate, and the cold indifference of the natural world. In its deceptively simple narrative, London manages to distill a powerful meditation on survival, instinct, hubris, and the limits of human knowledge.

The story follows an unnamed protagonist, a man traveling alone in the remote Yukon during an unforgiving winter. The temperature is unimaginably cold—far below zero—and yet the man presses forward, dismissing the advice of seasoned locals who warned him of the dangers of venturing out in such conditions. His only companion is a wolf-dog, whose instincts tell it to seek warmth and shelter rather than face the frozen wilderness. As the man struggles *To Build a Fire* to keep himself alive, each failure underscores his growing isolation, vulnerability, and ultimate insignificance against nature's overwhelming power.

To Build a Fire is not simply a story about one man's fight against freezing temperatures. It is a parable about humanity's fragile place in the universe, a reminder that nature is neither cruel nor kind, but simply indifferent. London, drawing from his own experiences in the Yukon during the Klondike Gold Rush, presents a landscape that is as beautiful as it is deadly. The snow, the ice, the bitter wind—these elements are not villains in a traditional sense, but they become forces that test the limits of human endurance and adaptability.

What sets this story apart from other survival narratives is London's stark, almost scientific tone. He does not romanticize the protagonist's struggle, nor does he suggest that nature will reward bravery or determination. Instead, he presents a world governed by natural laws, where survival depends not on heroic qualities but on one's ability to recognize and adapt to the realities of the environment. The man's downfall is not due to a lack of strength or intelligence but to his overconfidence and his disregard for the wisdom of experience—his belief that human ingenuity alone is enough to conquer the elements.

London's narrative style in *To Build a Fire* is a hallmark of literary naturalism, a movement that emerged in the late 19th century as a response to romanticism. Naturalist writers, influenced by scientific thought and Darwinian theory, sought to portray life as it is, often emphasizing the deterministic forces—heredity, environment, chance—that shape human destiny. In this story, London portrays the man's fate as a direct consequence of his environment and his inability to heed the warnings embedded in that environment. The cold is not an antagonist in the moral sense; it is simply a fact of life in the Yukon, and those who fail to respect it will not survive.

For readers approaching this story for the first time, it is worth noting the layers of meaning beneath its straightforward plot. On one level, it is a gripping tale of adventure and survival, full of vivid descriptions of the frozen landscape and the man's desperate attempts to keep warm. On another level, it is a philosophical reflection on the relationship between man and nature, reason and instinct, pride and humility. The contrast between the man and the dog is especially significant. While the man relies on reason and intellect, the dog survives by instinct and an innate understanding of the environment. In the end, it is the dog's instinct that prevails, underscoring London's belief in the primacy of nature's laws.

Themes of Hubris, Instinct, and the Power of Nature

One of the central themes of *To Build a Fire* is hubris—the fatal overconfidence of the protagonist. From the very beginning, the man ignores the advice of the "old-timer" from Sulphur Creek, who warned him never to travel alone in temperatures colder than fifty degrees below zero. The man's dismissal of this advice is not born of malice but of arrogance, a belief that he can outwit the natural world through sheer determination and cleverness. This belief proves to be his undoing, as each miscalculation brings him closer to disaster.

London portrays this hubris not as a personal flaw unique to the man but as a broader commentary on humanity's relationship with nature. In the modern age, we often assume that technology, intelligence, or willpower can overcome any obstacle. *To Build a Fire* challenges this assumption, reminding us that there are limits to human control and that survival often depends on humility and respect for forces beyond our control.

The story also contrasts human reason with animal instinct. The dog, though less intelligent in a human sense, understands the dangers of the extreme cold on a primal level. It senses that traveling in such conditions is dangerous and that survival depends on finding warmth and shelter. The man, by contrast, relies on his calculations and plans, failing to recognize that his intellectual approach cannot compensate for his lack of experience and respect for the environment. In this way, London suggests that instinct—rooted in thousands of years of adaptation—is often more reliable than human reasoning when it comes to survival in nature.

Another key theme is the power of the elements. London's descriptions of the Yukon winter are both beautiful and terrifying. The cold is described not just as a temperature but as a living presence, a force that seeps into the man's body and saps his strength. The act of building a fire, which gives the story its title, becomes a symbol of life itself—a fragile, flickering barrier between the man and certain death. When the man fails *To Build a Fire* at a crucial moment, it is not merely an accident; it is the collapse of his last defense against nature's overwhelming power.

London's depiction of nature is neither sentimental nor hostile. Nature is indifferent, operating according to its own laws, without regard for human desires or struggles. This indifference is what makes the story so powerful and so unsettling. The man's death is not a tragedy in the classical sense, because nature is not actively working against him. It simply does not care. This perspective aligns with the philosophy of naturalism, which emphasizes that human beings are subject to the same forces of chance and necessity as any other living creature.

The structure of the story reinforces these themes. London builds tension not through sudden shocks or dramatic confrontations but through a gradual accumulation of small mistakes and missed opportunities. Each time the man fails *To Build a Fire*, or underestimates the cold, the reader senses his margin for survival shrinking. The narrative moves inexorably toward its bleak conclusion, where the man, finally realizing the hopelessness of his situation, meets death with a mixture of regret and resignation.

The dog's survival at the end serves as a stark reminder of nature's impartiality. The dog is not heroic or sentimental; it simply acts according to its instincts, finding warmth and safety once the man is gone. In this sense, the story ends not with triumph or redemption but with a quiet affirmation of the natural order: those who adapt survive, and those who do not perish.

London's Legacy and the Reader's Experience

To Build a Fire is often considered Jack London's masterpiece, and for good reason. It is a story that combines vivid realism with profound philosophical insight, capturing the essence of London's worldview and literary style. Born in 1876, London lived a life of adventure and hardship, working as a sailor, gold prospector, and laborer before achieving success as a writer. His experiences in the Yukon during the Klondike Gold Rush provided the raw material for many of his most famous works, including *The Call of the Wild*, *White Fang*, and *To Build a Fire*.

London was deeply influenced by the ideas of Charles Darwin and the philosophy of naturalism. He believed that life was a struggle for survival, governed by the laws of nature and evolution. This belief is evident throughout *To Build a Fire*, where the man's fate is determined not by divine intervention or moral lessons but by his ability—or inability—to adapt to his environment.

For readers today, the story remains as relevant and compelling as it was when it was first published. Its themes of survival, humility, and respect for nature resonate in an era where human activity continues to challenge the limits of the natural world. The story serves as both a cautionary tale and a meditation on the timeless truths of existence.

When reading *To Build a Fire*, pay close attention to London's language and imagery. His descriptions of the Yukon landscape are not merely decorative; they create a palpable sense of place and mood, immersing the reader in the harsh, frozen environment. Notice how London uses sensory details—the crunch of snow, the sting of cold air, the flicker of a dying flame—to heighten the tension and bring the story to life.

Equally important is the psychological portrait of the protagonist. London does not name the man, a choice that makes him both universal and anonymous. He could be any person, any traveler who underestimates the power of nature. His thoughts and actions, though sometimes flawed, are presented with clarity and precision, allowing the reader to understand his motivations even as they foresee his doom.

The story's pacing is another aspect worth appreciating. London writes with a steady, measured rhythm, mirroring the man's journey through the snow. The moments of crisis—such as when the fire is extinguished by falling snow—are all the more powerful because they disrupt this rhythm, plunging the reader into the same sense of panic and urgency that grips the protagonist.

Ultimately, *To Build a Fire* invites readers to reflect on their own relationship with the natural world. It challenges us to consider how we might fare in similar circumstances, whether we would have the humility to respect the warnings of experience or the instincts to survive when reason fails.

It reminds us that nature is not an adversary to be conquered but a force to be understood and respected.

As you begin this story, allow yourself to be drawn into its stark, frozen landscape. Feel the bite of the cold, the desperation of the man's struggle, and the quiet, implacable presence of nature. Recognize that this is not just a story of one man's fate but a meditation on the universal truths of life, survival, and the fragile boundary between existence and oblivion.

To Build A Fire

The day had dawned cold and gray, extremely cold and gray, when the man left the main Yukon trail and climbed up the high earthen bank, where a faint and rarely used path led east through the thick spruce forest. The bank was steep, and he stopped to catch his breath at the top, justifying this pause by checking his watch. It was nine o'clock. There was no sun and no sign of the sun, even though the sky was completely clear of clouds. The day was bright, yet there seemed to be an invisible shroud covering everything, a mysterious darkness that dimmed the daylight, caused by the sun's absence. This situation didn't trouble the man. He had grown accustomed to living without sunlight. Days had passed since he had last seen the sun, and he understood that several more days would go by before that bright sphere, positioned to the south, would barely appear above the horizon before quickly disappearing again.

The man threw a glance back along the path he had traveled. The Yukon stretched a mile wide and lay buried beneath three feet of ice. Above this ice sat an equal depth of snow. Everything appeared pure white, rolling in smooth waves where the ice jams from the freeze had taken shape. To the north and south, as far as he could see, stretched unbroken white, except for a dark thin line that curved and wound from around the spruce-covered island to the south, and that bent and twisted away toward the north, where it vanished behind another spruce-covered island. This dark thin line was the trail—the main trail—that ran south five hundred miles to the Chilcoot Pass, Dyea, and salt water; and that ran north seventy miles to Dawson, and continued northward a thousand miles to Nulato, and eventually to St. Michael on Bering Sea, a thousand miles and half a thousand more.

But all this—the mysterious, far-reaching hairline trail, the absence of sun from the sky, the tremendous cold, and the strangeness and weirdness of it all—made no impression on the man. It wasn't because he had grown accustomed to it over time. He was a newcomer to the land, a chechaquo, and this was his first winter. His problem was that he lacked imagination. He was sharp and alert when it came to the practical matters of life, but only the practical matters, not their deeper meanings. Fifty degrees below zero meant eighty-some degrees of frost. This fact struck him as being cold and uncomfortable, and that was the extent of it. It didn't cause him to reflect on his vulnerability as a being dependent on temperature, or on humanity's fragility in general, able to survive only within certain narrow ranges of heat and cold; and from there it didn't lead him to contemplate the speculative realm of immortality and humanity's place in the universe. Fifty degrees below zero represented a biting frost that caused pain and had to be protected against by wearing mittens, ear-flaps, warm moccasins, and thick socks. Fifty degrees below zero was to him exactly fifty degrees below zero. The idea that there might be anything more to it than that never crossed his mind.

As he turned to continue walking, he spat thoughtfully. There was a sharp, explosive crackling sound that startled him. He spat once more. And again, while still in the air, before it could drop to the snow, his saliva crackled. He understood that when it was fifty degrees below zero, spit would crackle when it hit the snow, but this saliva had crackled while still airborne. Without question it was colder than fifty below—exactly how much colder he couldn't tell. But the temperature wasn't important. He was heading to the old mining claim on the left fork of Henderson Creek, where his companions were waiting. They had traveled over the mountain divide from the Indian Creek region, while he had taken the longer route to examine the potential for floating logs down from the Yukon islands come spring. He would reach camp by six o'clock; somewhat after sunset, certainly, but his friends would be there, a fire would be burning, and a warm dinner would be waiting. Regarding lunch, he pressed his palm against the bulging package beneath his coat. It was tucked under his shirt as well, bundled in a handkerchief and resting against his bare skin. This was the only method to prevent the biscuits from freezing solid. He grinned pleasantly to himself as he imagined those biscuits, each split open and soaked in bacon fat, and each containing a thick slice of fried bacon.

He dove into the thick grove of large spruce trees. The path was barely visible. About a foot of snow had accumulated since the last sled had traveled through, and he felt relieved that he wasn't pulling a sled and could move with minimal weight. Actually, he wasn't carrying anything except his lunch bundled up in a handkerchief. Still, the cold caught him off guard. It was definitely freezing, he realized, as he massaged his numb nose and cheekbones with his gloved hand. He had a full beard that kept him warm, but the facial hair couldn't shield his prominent cheekbones and his bold nose that jutted out boldly into the icy air.

Following closely behind the man was a dog, a large native husky—a true wolf-dog with a grey coat that showed no visible or behavioral differences from its wild wolf relatives. The extreme cold was weighing heavily on the animal. It sensed that this was not the right time to be traveling. The dog's natural instincts were telling it a more accurate story than the man's reasoning was telling him. In truth, the temperature wasn't just below fifty degrees below zero—it was colder than sixty below, colder than seventy below. The actual temperature was seventy-five degrees below zero. Given that the freezing point sits at thirty-two degrees above zero, this meant they were facing one hundred and seven degrees of frost. The dog had no understanding of thermometers. Perhaps its mind lacked the clear awareness of extreme cold that existed in the man's thoughts. However, the animal possessed its natural instincts. It felt an unclear yet threatening sense of danger that kept it subdued and caused it to creep along behind the man, making it watch anxiously for any unusual movement from him, as though anticipating that he might stop to make camp or find shelter somewhere and start a fire. The dog had come to understand fire, and it craved fire, or alternatively, the chance to dig into the snow and preserve its body heat away from the bitter air.

The frozen moisture from its breath had settled on its fur like a fine layer of frost, and its jowls, muzzle, and eyelashes were especially whitened by the crystallized breath. The man's red beard and mustache were also frosted, but more thickly, with the buildup forming ice that grew larger with each warm, moist breath he breathed out. The man was also chewing tobacco, and the ice covering his mouth held his lips so stiffly that he couldn't clear his chin when he spit out the juice. As a result, a crystal beard the color and thickness of amber was growing longer on his chin. If he fell down, it would break apart like glass into sharp pieces. But the strange attachment didn't bother him. It was the price all tobacco chewers paid in that region, and he had been out in two previous cold spells. Those hadn't been as cold as this one, he knew, but according to the alcohol thermometer at Sixty Mile, he knew they had recorded fifty below zero and fifty-five below.

He continued through the level stretch of woods for several miles, crossed a wide flat of tussocks, and descended down a bank to the frozen bed of a small stream. This was Henderson Creek, and he knew he was ten miles from the forks. He looked at his watch. It was ten o'clock. He was making four miles an hour, and he calculated that he would arrive at the forks at half-past twelve. He decided to celebrate that event by eating his lunch there.

The dog fell back into step behind him, its tail hanging low with dejection, as the man walked along the creek bottom. The groove left by the old sled trail could be clearly seen, but twelve inches of fresh snow had buried the tracks from the most recent runners. For an entire month, no one had traveled up or down this quiet creek. The man kept moving at a steady pace. He wasn't someone who spent much time thinking, and right now he especially had little to occupy his mind except that he planned to eat lunch at the forks and would reach camp with his companions by six o'clock. There was no one around to have a conversation with, and even if there had been, talking would have been impossible due to the ice covering that had formed over his mouth. So he kept mechanically chewing his tobacco and adding to the length of his amber-colored beard.

Every so often the thought came back to him that it was extremely cold and that he had never felt cold like this before. While walking, he rubbed his cheekbones and nose with the back of his mittened hand. He did this without thinking, occasionally switching hands. But no matter how much he rubbed, the moment he stopped his cheekbones would go numb, and right after that the tip of his nose would go numb. He was definitely going to get frostbite on his cheeks; he knew this, and felt a stab of regret that he hadn't made a nose-guard like the kind Bud wore during cold spells. That kind of guard went across the cheeks too, protecting them as well. But it wasn't really that important, when you thought about it. What did frostbitten cheeks matter? They hurt a little, that was all; they were never anything serious.

Although the man's mind was empty of thoughts, he remained keenly observant, noticing the changes in the creek, the curves and bends and fallen timber, and he always paid careful attention to where he placed his feet. At one point, coming around a bend, he suddenly pulled back like a startled horse, veering away from where he had been walking and backing up several steps along the trail. He knew the creek was frozen solid all the way to the bottom— no creek could hold water in that arctic winter—but he also knew there were springs that bubbled up from the hillsides and flowed beneath the snow and on top of the creek's ice. He understood that even the coldest weather never froze these springs, and he was equally aware of their danger. They were traps. They concealed pools of water under the snow that could be three inches deep or three feet deep. Sometimes a thin layer of ice, half an inch thick, covered them, which was then covered by snow. Sometimes there were alternating layers of water and thin ice, so that when someone broke through, they would keep breaking through for some time, sometimes getting soaked up to the waist.

That was why he had jumped back in such terror. He had felt the ground give way beneath his feet and heard the crackling sound of ice covered by snow. Getting his feet wet in temperatures like this spelled trouble and danger. At minimum, it would mean a delay, since he would have to stop and build a fire, then take shelter behind it while he removed his boots to dry his socks and footwear. He stood there examining the creek bed and its banks, then determined that the water was flowing from the right. He thought for a moment, rubbing his nose and cheeks, then moved around to the left, walking carefully and testing each step before putting his full weight down. Once he was past the dangerous area, he took a fresh piece of chewing tobacco and resumed his steady four-mile-per-hour pace.

Over the next two hours, he encountered several more of these dangerous traps. Most of the time, the snow covering the concealed pools looked sunken and crystallized, clearly warning of the hazard beneath. However, he had another narrow escape, and on one occasion, sensing potential danger, he forced the dog to walk ahead of him. The dog was reluctant to proceed. It hesitated until the man pushed it forward, then it moved swiftly across the white, undisturbed surface. Without warning, it plunged through, struggled to one side, and managed to reach more solid ground. Its front paws and legs had gotten wet, and almost instantly the water clinging to them froze into ice. The dog quickly tried to lick the ice from its legs, then lay down in the snow and started biting out the ice that had accumulated between its toes. This behavior was purely instinctual. Allowing the ice to stay would result in painful, injured feet. The dog didn't understand this reasoning. It simply followed the mysterious impulse that emerged from the deepest recesses of its nature. But the man understood, having formed an opinion about the situation, and he took off the mitten from his right hand to help remove the ice fragments. He kept his fingers exposed for no more than a minute, yet he was shocked by how quickly numbness struck them. The cold was truly severe. He quickly put the mitten back on and vigorously beat his hand against his chest.

At twelve o'clock the day reached its brightest point. However, the sun was too far south in its winter path to rise above the horizon. The curve of the earth blocked it from Henderson Creek, where the man walked beneath a clear sky at midday without casting any shadow. At exactly half-past twelve, he reached the place where the creek split into two branches. He felt satisfied with how fast he had traveled. If he maintained this pace, he would definitely join his companions by six o'clock. He unfastened his jacket and shirt and pulled out his lunch. This movement took less than fifteen seconds, but in that short time the cold seized his bare fingers. He didn't put his mitten back on, but instead hit his fingers hard against his leg a dozen times. Then he sat down on a log covered with snow to eat his meal. The sharp pain that came from striking his fingers against his leg disappeared so suddenly that it surprised him—he hadn't even had time to take a bite of his biscuit. He hit his fingers over and over again and put them back in the mitten, then exposed his other hand so he could eat. He attempted to take a bite, but the ice covering his mouth got in the way. He had forgotten to make a fire and let everything thaw. He laughed at his mistake, and while laughing he noticed the numbness spreading through his exposed fingers. He also realized that the stinging sensation that had started in his toes when he first sat down was already fading. He questioned whether his toes felt warm or had gone numb. He wiggled them inside his moccasins and concluded that they had lost feeling.

He quickly pulled on the mitten and got to his feet. Fear crept through him. He stomped back and forth until the sharp sensation returned to his feet. It was definitely cold, he realized. That fellow from Sulphur Creek had been telling the truth when he described how frigid it could get in this region. And he had actually laughed at the man back then! This proved that a person shouldn't be overly confident about things. There was absolutely no doubt about it—it was freezing. He paced back and forth, stomping his feet and swinging his arms around, until the returning warmth gave him comfort. Then he took out his matches and began building a fire. From the brush, where the high waters from last spring had left behind a collection of dried branches, he gathered his fuel. Starting small and working with care, he quickly built a crackling fire that melted the ice from his face and provided shelter while he ate his biscuits. For now, he had outsmarted the bitter cold of the wilderness. The dog found comfort in the flames, positioning itself close enough to feel the heat but far enough back to avoid getting burned.

When the man had finished, he filled his pipe and took his time enjoying a leisurely smoke. Then he put on his mittens, pulled the ear-flaps of his cap securely around his ears, and headed up the creek trail toward the left fork. The dog felt disappointed and longed to return to the fire. This man didn't understand cold. Perhaps all the generations of his ancestors had never experienced cold, genuine cold, cold that reached one hundred and seven degrees below freezing. But the dog understood; all its ancestors understood, and it had inherited this knowledge. And it knew that venturing out in such terrible cold was dangerous. This was the time to stay warm and hidden in a snow burrow and wait for clouds to cover the sky from where this bitter cold descended. However, there existed a close bond between the dog and the man. One served as the laboring servant of the other, and the only affection it had ever known came from the sting of the whip and harsh, threatening sounds that promised more lashing. So the dog made no attempt to share its fear with the man. It wasn't worried about the man's safety; it longed for the fire purely for its own comfort. But the man whistled and called to it with sounds like whip-cracks, and the dog fell into step behind the man and followed along.

The man took a bite of tobacco and began forming a fresh amber-colored beard of juice. His warm breath also quickly frosted his mustache, eyebrows, and eyelashes with white crystals. There appeared to be fewer springs along the left branch of the Henderson, and for thirty minutes the man observed no evidence of any. Then it occurred. At a spot where no warning signs existed, where the smooth, undisturbed snow appeared to promise solid ground underneath, the man fell through. The depth wasn't significant. He soaked himself up to mid-thigh before he struggled back onto the solid surface.

He was furious and cursed his bad luck out loud. He had planned to reach camp with the other men by six o'clock, and this setback would cost him an hour since he'd need *To Build a Fire* and dry his boots. At such freezing temperatures, this was absolutely necessary—he understood that much—so he turned toward the riverbank and climbed up. At the top, caught in the brush around several small spruce trees, lay a pile of dry firewood left by high water—mostly sticks and twigs, but also some larger pieces of weathered branches and fine, dry grass from the previous year. He tossed several big pieces down onto the snow. This created a base that would keep the new flame from extinguishing itself in the snow it would otherwise melt. He started the flame by striking a match against a small piece of birch bark he pulled from his pocket. This caught fire even faster than paper would have. Setting it on his foundation, he nourished the growing flame with strands of dry grass and the smallest dry twigs he could find.

He worked slowly and carefully, acutely conscious of the peril he faced. Little by little, as the flame grew stronger, he added larger twigs to feed it. He crouched in the snow, extracting the twigs from where they were tangled in the brush and placing them directly into the flame. He understood there could be no mistake. When the temperature drops to seventy-five degrees below zero, a man cannot afford to fail in his first attempt at building a fire—especially if his feet are wet. If his feet are dry and he fails, he can jog along the trail for half a mile and get his blood flowing again. But when it's seventy-five below, running cannot restore circulation to wet and freezing feet. Regardless of how quickly he runs, the wet feet will only freeze more severely.

The man was aware of all this. The old-timer from Sulphur Creek had warned him about it the previous fall, and now he was truly understanding that advice. He had already lost all feeling in his feet. Building the fire had required him to take off his mittens, and his fingers had quickly become numb. Walking at four miles per hour had kept his heart pumping blood to his body's surface and to all his extremities. But the moment he stopped, his heart's pumping action slowed down. The cold of space struck the exposed tip of the planet, and since he was on that exposed tip, he took the full impact of that blow. His body's blood pulled back from it. The blood was alive, just like the dog, and like the dog, it wanted to retreat and protect itself from the terrible cold. As long as he maintained his four-mile-per-hour pace, he forced that blood to the surface whether he wanted to or not; but now it flowed away and retreated into the deeper parts of his body. His extremities were the first to notice its absence. His wet feet froze more quickly, and his exposed fingers became numb more rapidly, even though they hadn't started freezing yet. His nose and cheeks were already freezing, while the skin across his entire body grew cold as it lost its blood supply.

But he was safe. The frost would only nip his toes, nose, and cheeks, since the fire was starting to burn strongly. He fed it with twigs about the size of his finger. In another minute he'd be able to add branches as thick as his wrist, and then he could take off his wet footwear and keep his bare feet warm by the fire while they dried, rubbing them with snow at first, naturally. The fire was working perfectly. He was safe. He recalled the old-timer's advice from Sulphur Creek and grinned. The old-timer had been dead serious about his rule that no man should travel alone in the Klondike when it's fifty below or colder. Well, here he was; he'd had his accident; he was by himself; and he'd managed to save himself. Some of those old-timers were pretty much like worried women, he figured. All a man needed to do was stay calm, and everything would work out fine. Any real man could handle traveling solo. But it was startling how quickly his cheeks and nose were starting to freeze. And he hadn't expected his fingers to become numb so fast. They were completely numb now, since he could barely get them to work together to grab a twig, and they felt disconnected from his body and himself. When he picked up a twig, he had to watch to see if he actually had a grip on it. The connection between him and his fingertips was almost completely cut off.

None of this mattered much. The fire was there, crackling and popping, each dancing flame offering the promise of life. He began working to remove his moccasins. Ice covered them completely; his heavy German socks had become like metal sheaths reaching halfway up his legs; the moccasin laces felt like twisted steel rods, tangled and knotted as if they'd been through a blazing fire. He struggled briefly with his numb fingers, then, understanding how pointless this was, he pulled out his sheath knife.

But before he could cut the strings, it happened. It was his own fault or, rather, his mistake. He should not have built the fire under the spruce tree. He should have built it in the open. But it had been easier to pull the twigs from the brush and drop them directly on the fire. Now the tree under which he had done this carried a weight of snow on its boughs. No wind had blown for weeks, and each bough was fully loaded. Each time he had pulled a twig he had sent a slight tremor through the tree—an almost invisible tremor, as far as he was concerned, but a tremor strong enough to bring about the disaster. High up in the tree one branch dumped its load of snow. This fell on the branches beneath, causing them to dump theirs. This process continued, spreading out and involving the whole tree. It grew like an avalanche, and it descended without warning upon the man and the fire, and the fire was extinguished! Where it had burned was a blanket of fresh and scattered snow.

The man was stunned. It felt like he had just received his death sentence. For a moment he sat there, staring at the place where the fire had been burning. Then he became very calm. Maybe the old-timer from Sulphur Creek had been right. If only he'd had a traveling companion, he wouldn't be in danger right now. His partner could have built the fire. Well, it was his responsibility to build the fire again, and this time he couldn't afford to fail. Even if he managed to succeed, he would probably lose some toes. His feet had to be severely frostbitten by now, and it would take time before the second fire would be ready.

These thoughts raced through his mind, but he didn't just sit there dwelling on them. While his mind churned with these ideas, his body stayed busy—he built a new base for a fire, this time out in the open where no treacherous tree could snuff it out. Then he collected dry grass and small twigs from the debris left by high water. His fingers wouldn't bend enough to pick them out individually, but he managed to scoop them up by the handful. This method meant he ended up with plenty of rotten twigs and chunks of green moss that he didn't want, but it was the best he could manage. He worked systematically, even gathering an armload of larger branches to use later once the fire grew stronger. Throughout this entire process, the dog sat watching him with a certain longing wistfulness in its eyes, because it saw him as the one who brought fire, and the fire was taking too long to appear.

When everything was prepared, the man reached into his pocket for another piece of birch bark. He knew the bark was in there, and although he couldn't feel it with his fingers, he could hear it rustling crisply as he searched for it. No matter how hard he tried, he couldn't get a grip on it. Meanwhile, he remained constantly aware that his feet were freezing with each passing moment. This realization threatened to send him into a panic, but he resisted the urge and stayed composed. He used his teeth to pull on his mittens and swung his arms back and forth, striking his hands against his sides with all the force he could muster. He performed these movements both sitting and standing, while the entire time the dog remained seated in the snow, its bushy wolf-like tail curled warmly around its front paws, its pointed wolf ears standing alert as it observed the man intently. As the man continued beating and swinging his arms and hands, he felt a powerful wave of jealousy when he looked at the animal that stayed warm and protected in its natural coat.

After some time, he became aware of the first distant signals of feeling returning to his battered fingers. The faint tingling grew stronger until it developed into a sharp, burning pain that was agonizing, but which the man welcomed with relief. He pulled the mitten from his right hand and brought out the birch bark. The exposed fingers were rapidly becoming numb again. Next he pulled out his bundle of sulfur matches. But the extreme cold had already drained the life from his fingers. As he tried to separate one match from the rest, the entire bundle dropped into the snow. He attempted to pick it out of the snow, but couldn't manage it. The lifeless fingers could neither feel nor grasp. He remained very cautious. He pushed thoughts of his freezing feet, nose, and cheeks from his mind, focusing his entire attention on the matches. He observed carefully, relying on his sight instead of touch, and when he saw his fingers positioned on either side of the bundle, he closed them—or rather, he intended to close them, because while the mental command was sent, his fingers refused to respond. He slipped the mitten back onto his right hand and struck it hard against his knee. Then, using both mittened hands, he gathered up the bundle of matches along with a good amount of snow into his lap. Still, his situation hadn't improved.

After some maneuvering, he managed to grip the bundle between the heels of his gloved hands. He brought it to his mouth this way. The ice made crackling and snapping sounds as he forced his mouth open with great effort. He pulled his lower jaw down, pushed his upper lip aside, and used his upper teeth to scrape against the bundle to pull out a single match. He successfully extracted one, but it fell onto his lap. This didn't improve his situation at all. He couldn't pick it up with his hands. Then he came up with a solution. He grasped it between his teeth and struck it against his leg. He scraped it twenty times before he finally got it to light. Once it burst into flame, he held it in his teeth against the birch bark. However, the burning sulfur traveled up into his nose and down into his lungs, making him cough violently. The match dropped into the snow and died out.

The old-timer on Sulphur Creek had been right, he realized in that moment of controlled despair that followed: when temperatures drop below fifty degrees below zero, a man should never travel alone. He pounded his hands together, but couldn't feel anything. Without warning, he exposed both hands, pulling off the mittens with his teeth. He grabbed the entire bundle of matches between the palms of his hands. Since his arm muscles weren't frozen, he was able to press his palms firmly against the matches. Then he struck the whole bundle against his leg. The matches burst into flames—all seventy sulfur matches igniting at once! No wind threatened to extinguish them. He turned his head away to avoid the choking smoke and held the burning bundle against the birch bark. As he held it there, he began to notice feeling returning to his hand. His skin was burning. He could smell the flesh cooking. Far beneath the surface, he could feel it happening. The feeling transformed into pain that became increasingly sharp. Yet he continued to bear it, awkwardly holding the flaming matches against the bark that refused to catch fire easily because his own burning hands blocked the way, soaking up most of the flame.

Finally, when he couldn't bear it any longer, he pulled his hands apart. The burning matches dropped hissing into the snow, but the birch bark had caught fire. He started placing dry grass and the smallest twigs onto the flame. He couldn't be selective, since he had to lift the fuel using the heels of his hands. Bits of decayed wood and green moss stuck to the twigs, and he gnawed them off as best he could with his teeth. He tended the flame with great care but clumsily. It represented life, and it couldn't be allowed to die. As blood retreated from his body's surface, he began to shake, becoming even more clumsy. A large chunk of green moss dropped directly onto the small fire. He attempted to push it away with his fingers, but his trembling body caused him to push too hard, and he destroyed the center of the small fire, scattering the burning grass and tiny twigs. He attempted to gather them back together, but despite his intense concentration, his shivering overcame him, and the twigs scattered beyond hope. Each twig released a small cloud of smoke and died out. The fire-maker had been defeated. As he gazed listlessly around him, his eyes happened upon the dog, sitting beyond the remains of the fire from him, in the snow, making restless, hunching motions, gently raising one front paw and then the other, shifting its weight between them with longing anticipation.

The sight of the dog sparked a desperate idea in his mind. He recalled the story of a man trapped in a blizzard who killed a steer and crawled inside its carcass to survive. He would kill the dog and plunge his hands into the warm body until feeling returned to them. Then he could start another fire. He called to the dog, trying to coax it closer, but his voice carried an unfamiliar tone of fear that alarmed the animal, who had never heard the man speak this way before. Something was wrong, and the dog's instincts detected danger—it couldn't identify what kind of threat, but somewhere in its mind, a wariness of the man began to form. The dog flattened its ears at the sound of the man's voice, and its restless, crouching movements and the lifting and shifting of its front paws became more noticeable, but it refused to approach the man. He dropped to his hands and knees and crawled toward the dog. This strange behavior heightened the animal's suspicion, and it stepped carefully away.

The man sat up in the snow for a moment and fought to regain his composure. Then he pulled on his mittens using his teeth and stood up. He looked down first to make sure he was actually standing, since he couldn't feel his feet and felt disconnected from the ground. His upright posture began to ease the dog's suspicions, and when he spoke commandingly with a sharp, whip-like tone in his voice, the dog showed its usual obedience and approached him. As it came close enough to reach, the man lost control of himself. His arms shot out toward the dog, and he felt genuine shock when he realized his hands couldn't grip anything, that his fingers had no flexibility or sensation. He had momentarily forgotten that they were frozen and becoming more frozen by the minute. All of this happened rapidly, and before the animal could escape, he wrapped his arms around its body. He sat down in the snow and held the dog this way while it growled and whimpered and fought to break free.

But that was all he could manage—holding the dog's body wrapped in his arms while sitting there. He understood that killing the dog was impossible for him. There was simply no way he could do it. His useless hands couldn't draw or grip his sheath knife, nor could he strangle the creature. He let the dog go, and it bolted away frantically with its tail tucked between its legs, still growling. The animal stopped about forty feet away and watched him with curiosity, its ears standing straight up and alert. The man glanced down at his hands to figure out where they were and discovered them dangling at the ends of his arms. He found it strange that he needed to look with his eyes to determine where his hands were located. He started swinging his arms back and forth forcefully, slapping his mittened hands against his sides. He continued this vigorous motion for five minutes, and his heart pumped sufficient blood to the surface to stop his shivering. However, he felt no sensation in his hands whatsoever. He sensed that they hung like dead weights at the ends of his arms, but when he attempted to focus on this feeling, he couldn't grasp it.

A dull, oppressive fear of death settled over him. This fear quickly intensified as he understood that this was no longer simply about freezing his fingers and toes, or losing his hands and feet, but about life and death with the odds stacked against him. This realization sent him into a panic, and he spun around and ran up the creek bed along the old, faded trail. The dog fell in behind him and matched his pace. He ran without thinking, without purpose, gripped by a terror unlike anything he had ever experienced in his life. Gradually, as he struggled and stumbled through the snow, he began to notice his surroundings again—the creek banks, the old logjams, the bare aspens, and the sky above. Running made him feel better. He stopped shivering. Perhaps, if he kept running, his feet would warm up; and besides, if he ran far enough, he would reach camp and his companions. He would certainly lose some fingers and toes and parts of his face; but his friends would care for him and save what remained of him when he arrived. Yet at the same time, another thought lurked in his mind, telling him he would never reach the camp and his companions; that it was too many miles away, that the cold had gained too much ground on him, and that he would soon be frozen and dead. He pushed this thought into the background and refused to acknowledge it. Sometimes it forced its way forward and demanded attention, but he shoved it back and tried to focus on other things.

It seemed strange to him that he could run at all on feet so numb from cold that he couldn't feel them hitting the ground or supporting his body weight. He felt like he was gliding just above the surface, completely disconnected from the earth beneath him. He remembered seeing an image of winged Mercury somewhere before, and he wondered if Mercury experienced this same sensation when flying over the earth.

His plan to run all the way back to camp where the boys were waiting had a serious problem: he didn't have enough stamina. He stumbled multiple times, and eventually he swayed, collapsed, and hit the ground. When he attempted to get back up, he couldn't manage it. He decided he needed to sit down and rest, and the next time he would simply walk steadily instead of running. While he sat there catching his breath, he realized he was feeling surprisingly warm and comfortable. He wasn't shivering anymore, and it felt like a pleasant warmth had spread through his chest and torso. However, when he touched his nose or cheeks, he couldn't feel anything at all. Running wouldn't bring feeling back to them. It wouldn't restore sensation to his hands and feet either. Then it occurred to him that the frozen parts of his body were probably spreading. He attempted to push this thought away, to ignore it, to focus on something different; he recognized the surge of panic it triggered, and he feared giving in to that panic. But the thought forced its way back, continuing to plague him, until it created a mental image of his entire body frozen solid. This was unbearable, and he took off in another frantic sprint down the trail. When he eventually slowed to a walk, the idea of the freezing spreading further through his body made him break into a run once more.

The dog stayed right beside him the entire time, running at his heels. When he collapsed for the second time, the dog curled its tail over its front paws and sat directly in front of him, watching with curious eagerness and focused attention. The animal's warmth and sense of safety made him angry, and he swore at it until it pressed its ears down in submission. This time the trembling overtook the man much faster. He was losing his fight against the freezing cold. The frost was seeping into his body from every direction. The realization pushed him forward, but he managed to run only about a hundred feet before he stumbled and fell face-first into the snow. This was his final moment of terror. After he caught his breath and regained his composure, he sat up and began to consider the idea of facing death with honor. Yet this concept didn't present itself to him in those exact words. What he actually thought was that he had been acting like an idiot, racing around like a headless chicken—that was the comparison that came to mind. Since he was going to freeze to death regardless, he figured he might as well accept it with some grace. Along with this newfound sense of calm came the first hints of sleepiness. Sleeping his way into death seemed like a reasonable plan, he decided. It would be similar to receiving anesthesia. Dying from cold wasn't as terrible as most people believed. There were certainly much worse ways to die.

He imagined the boys discovering his body the following day. All at once he found himself alongside them, walking down the trail and searching for himself. And, remaining with them, he rounded a bend in the trail and discovered himself lying in the snow. He no longer belonged with himself, because even then he had separated from himself, standing with the boys and observing himself in the snow. It was definitely cold, he thought. When he returned to the States he would be able to tell people what genuine cold felt like. His mind wandered from this to an image of the old-timer on Sulphur Creek. He could picture him clearly, warm and cozy, smoking a pipe.

"You were right, old friend; you were right," the man mumbled to the old-timer of Sulphur Creek.

Then the man drifted off into what felt like the most comfortable and satisfying sleep he had ever experienced. The dog sat facing him and waiting. The short day came to an end in a long, slow twilight. There were no signs of a fire being built, and besides, never in the dog's experience had it seen a man sit like that in the snow without making a fire. As the twilight continued, its eager longing for the fire overcame it, and with a great lifting and shifting of its front paws, it whined softly, then flattened its ears down expecting to be scolded by the man. But the man stayed silent. Later, the dog whined loudly. And even later it crept close to the man and picked up the scent of death. This made the animal's fur stand on end and caused it to back away. A little longer it waited, howling under the stars that jumped and danced and shone brilliantly in the cold sky. Then it turned and trotted up the trail toward the camp it knew, where the other food-providers and fire-providers were.

That Spot

I don't have much respect for Stephen Mackaye anymore, even though I used to believe in him completely. I know that back then I loved him more than my own brother. If I ever run into Stephen Mackaye again, I won't be able to control what I might do. It's beyond my understanding how a man I shared meals and shelter with, and who traveled with me over the Chilcoot Trail, could end up the way he has. I always judged Steve to be an honest man, a caring friend, without a trace of spite or cruelty in his character. I'll never trust my ability to judge people again. I mean, I took care of that man when he had typhoid fever; we went hungry together at the headwaters of the Stewart; and he saved my life on the Little Salmon. And now, after all the years we spent together, all I can say about Stephen Mackaye is that he's the most despicable person I've ever known.

We headed for the Klondike during the fall rush of 1897, but we started too late to make it over Chilcoot Pass before everything froze up. We carried our supplies on our backs for part of the journey, but when the snow started falling, we had to buy dogs to pull our gear the rest of the way on sleds. That's how we ended up with that dog Spot. Dogs were expensive, and we paid one hundred and ten dollars for him. He certainly looked like he was worth every penny. I say looked because he was one of the most impressive dogs I'd ever laid eyes on. He weighed sixty pounds and had all the physical traits of an excellent sled dog. We could never figure out exactly what breed he was. He wasn't a husky, Malemute, or Hudson Bay dog; he resembled all of them yet didn't quite match any of them perfectly. On top of that, he clearly had some domestic dog mixed in his bloodline, because on one side of his body, cutting through the blend of yellow-brown-red-and-dirty-white that made up his main coloring, there was a coal-black patch as large as a water bucket. That's exactly why we named him Spot.

He was definitely handsome. When he was in good shape, his muscles bulged out in clusters all across his body. He was the most powerful-looking animal I'd ever seen in Alaska, and also appeared to be the most intelligent. Just looking at him, you'd assume he could outpull three dogs of his own weight. Perhaps he could have, but I never witnessed it. His intelligence didn't work in that direction. He could steal and scavenge flawlessly; he possessed an instinct that was downright eerie for sensing when work needed to be done and for sneaking away accordingly; and when it came to getting lost and then finding his way back, he was absolutely brilliant. However, when it came to actual work, the way his intelligence would drain away from him and leave him as nothing more than a quivering, mindless mess would break your heart.

There are times when I think it wasn't stupidity. Maybe, like some men I know, he was too smart to work. I wouldn't be surprised if he outsmarted us all with that intelligence of his. Maybe he figured it all out and decided that getting beaten now and then without having to work was much better than working all the time without getting beaten. He was intelligent enough for that kind of calculation. I'm telling you, I've sat and stared into that dog's eyes until shivers ran up and down my spine and my bones felt like they were crawling with yeast, because of the intelligence I saw shining out. I can't put into words what I mean about that intelligence. It's beyond ordinary language. I saw it, that's all. Sometimes it was like looking into a human soul when I looked into his eyes; and what I saw there scared me and got me thinking about reincarnation and all that stuff. I'm telling you I felt something powerful in that animal's eyes; there was a message there, but I wasn't capable enough to understand it. Whatever it was (I know I sound like an idiot)—whatever it was, it confused me completely. I can't give you even a hint of what I saw in that animal's eyes; it wasn't light, it wasn't color; it was something that moved, way back deep, when the eyes themselves weren't moving. And I don't think I actually saw it move either; I just felt that it moved. It was an expression—that's what it was— and I got a sense of it. No; it was different from just an expression; it was more than that. I don't know what it was, but it gave me a feeling of connection all the same. Oh, no, not emotional connection. It was more like a connection of equals. Those eyes never begged like a deer's eyes. They challenged. No, it wasn't rebellion. It was just a quiet assumption of equality. And I don't think it was intentional. I believe it was unconscious on his part. It was there because it was there, and it couldn't help showing through. No, I don't mean showing. It didn't show; it moved. I know I'm talking nonsense, but if you'd looked into that animal's eyes the way I have, you'd understand. Steve was affected the same way I was. Why, I tried to kill that Spot once—he was useless for anything; and I couldn't go through with it. I led him out into the woods, and he came along slowly and reluctantly. He knew what was happening. I stopped in a good spot, put my foot on the rope, and drew my big Colt. And that dog sat down and looked at me. I'm telling you he didn't beg. He just looked. And I saw all kinds of mysterious things moving, yes, moving, in those eyes of his. I didn't actually see them move; I thought I saw them, because, like I said before, I think I only sensed them. And I want to tell you right now that it was too much for me. It was like killing a man, a aware, brave man, who looked calmly at your gun as if to say, "Who's afraid?"

Then, too, the message seemed so close that instead of quickly pulling the trigger, I paused to see if I could grasp what he was trying to tell me. There it was, right in front of me, shining all around in those eyes of his. And then it was too late. I became frightened. I was shaking all over, and my stomach developed a nervous flutter that made me feel nauseous. I simply sat down and stared at the dog, and he stared back at me, until I thought I was losing my mind. Do you want to know what I did? I dropped the gun and ran back to camp with the fear of God in my heart. Steve laughed at me. But I noticed that Steve took Spot into the woods a week later for the same purpose, and that Steve returned alone, and a little while later Spot wandered back as well.

Regardless, Spot refused to work. We had spent one hundred and ten dollars for him from our meager funds, and he simply wouldn't work. He wouldn't even pull against the harness straps. Steve spoke to him the first time we harnessed him up, and he just trembled slightly, nothing more. Not an ounce of pull on the traces. He simply stood there and shook, like a mass of jelly. Steve tapped him with the whip. He yelped, but still not an ounce of effort. Steve struck him again, somewhat harder, and he howled—that distinctive long wolf howl. Then Steve lost his temper and whipped him half a dozen times, and I came running from the tent.

I told Steve he was being cruel to the animal, and we got into an argument—the first disagreement we'd ever had. He threw the whip down in the snow and stormed off angrily. I picked it up and took over. That dog Spot started shaking and trembling and cringing even before I raised the whip, and when the first strike hit him he cried out like a tortured soul. Then he collapsed in the snow. I got the other dogs moving, and they pulled him along while I kept hitting him with the whip. He flipped onto his back and bounced along the ground, his four legs flailing in the air, howling as if he was being put through a meat grinder. Steve returned and started laughing at me, so I apologized for what I had said.

There was no way to get any work out of that Spot, and to compensate for it, he was the biggest glutton of a dog I've ever encountered. On top of that, he was the most cunning thief. There was no way to outsmart him. We went without bacon for breakfast many times because Spot had gotten there before us. And it was his fault that we nearly starved to death up the Stewart. He figured out how to break into our meat storage, and whatever he didn't eat, the rest of the team devoured. But he was fair about it. He stole from everyone. He was a restless dog, always busy nosing around or heading somewhere. And there wasn't a camp within five miles that he didn't pillage. The worst part was that they always came back to us demanding payment for his meals, which was fair according to local custom, but it was extremely difficult for us, especially that first winter on the Chilcoot, when we were broke and paying for entire hams and slabs of bacon that we never got to eat. That Spot could fight too. He could do anything except work. He never pulled a single pound, but he dominated the entire team. The way he made those dogs submit was quite a sight to see. He intimidated them, and there was always one or more of them bearing fresh marks from his teeth. But he was more than just a bully. He wasn't scared of anything that moved on four legs, and I've watched him march alone into an unfamiliar team, without any reason at all, and completely defeat the whole group. Did I mention he could eat? I once caught him eating the whip. That's the truth. He started with the leather tip, and when I found him he had worked his way down to the handle and was still chewing.

But he was handsome. At the end of the first week, we sold him for seventy-five dollars to the Mounted Police. They had experienced dog handlers, and we knew that by the time he had traveled the six hundred miles to Dawson, he would be an excellent sled dog. I say we knew, because we were just beginning to get familiar with that Spot. A little later, we weren't bold enough to claim we knew anything when it came to him. A week later, we woke up in the morning to the most incredible dog fight we had ever heard. It was that Spot who had returned and was getting the team back in line. We ate a rather gloomy breakfast, I can tell you; but our spirits lifted two hours later when we sold him to an official courier who was heading to Dawson with government dispatches. That Spot took only three days to come back, and as always, he marked his return with a brawl.

We spent the winter and spring after our own equipment was transported across the pass, hauling other people's supplies, and we made a substantial profit. We also earned money from Spot. If we sold him once, we sold him twenty times. He always returned, and no one demanded their money back. We didn't want the money. We would have paid generously for anyone to take him off our hands permanently. We had to get rid of him, and we couldn't give him away, because that would have seemed suspicious. But he was such a handsome-looking animal that we never had any trouble selling him. "Unbroken," we'd tell them, and they'd pay whatever price for him. We sold him for as little as twenty-five dollars, and once we received a hundred and fifty for him. That specific buyer brought him back in person, refused to take his money back, and the way he berated us was absolutely terrible. He said it was worth the price just to tell us what he thought of us, and we felt he was so right that we never argued back. But to this day I've never completely recovered all the self-respect I had before that man spoke to me.

When the ice cleared from the lakes and river, we loaded our equipment into a Lake Bennett boat and headed for Dawson. We had an excellent team of dogs, and naturally we placed them on top of our gear. That dog Spot came with us—there was no way to get rid of him; and at least a dozen times on the first day alone, he knocked one dog after another overboard while fighting with them. The space was cramped, and he couldn't stand being pressed in so tightly.

"That dog needs some room to roam," Steve said on the second day. "Let's leave him stranded somewhere."

We did exactly that, steering the boat to shore at Caribou Crossing so he could leap off. Two of our other dogs, both excellent animals, went after him, and we wasted two entire days searching for them. We never laid eyes on those two dogs again, but the peace and calm we experienced afterward convinced us, much like the man who turned down his hundred and fifty dollars, that it was worth every bit of trouble. For the first time in months, Steve and I found ourselves laughing, whistling, and singing. We felt as content as could be. The difficult times had passed. The terrible ordeal had finally ended. Spot was gone.

Three weeks later, one morning, Steve and I were standing on the riverbank at Dawson. A small boat had just arrived from Lake Bennett. I saw Steve jolt suddenly, and heard him mutter something unpleasant under his breath.

Then I looked over, and there, sitting in the front of the boat with his ears perked up, was Spot. Steve and I immediately slipped away like beaten dogs, like cowards, like criminals fleeing from justice. This last comparison was exactly what the police lieutenant thought when he spotted us sneaking around. He assumed there were law enforcement officers on the boat who were pursuing us. He didn't bother to investigate further, but kept us in his sight, and cornered us in the M. & M. saloon. We had quite a time trying to explain ourselves, since we refused to return to the boat and face Spot; eventually he kept us under the watch of another policeman while he went to check the boat himself. After we managed to get away from him, we headed back to the cabin, and when we got there, Spot was sitting on the front steps waiting for us. Now how did he figure out where we lived? There were forty thousand people in Dawson that summer, and how did he pick out our cabin from all the other cabins? How did he even know we were in Dawson in the first place? I leave that question to you. But don't forget what I mentioned about his intelligence and that eternal something I've seen flickering in his eyes.

There was no way to get rid of him anymore. Too many people in Dawson had bought him drinks up on Chilcoot, and word had spread around town. We put him on steamboats heading down the Yukon at least six times, but he would simply get off at the first stop and walk back up the riverbank. We couldn't sell him, we couldn't kill him (both Steve and I had attempted it), and no one else could kill him either. He seemed to live under some kind of magical protection. I witnessed him get caught in a dog fight on the main street with fifty dogs piled on top of him, and when they were pulled apart, he would emerge standing on all four legs without a scratch, while two of the dogs that had been attacking him would be lying there dead.

I watched him steal a piece of moose meat from Major Dinwiddie's storage cache that was so heavy he could barely stay one step ahead of Mrs. Dinwiddie's Native cook, who was chasing him with an axe. As he ran up the hill, after the cook gave up the chase, Major Dinwiddie himself came outside and fired his Winchester rifle wildly across the area. He emptied his ammunition magazine twice and never hit that dog Spot once. Then a police officer arrived and arrested him for firing weapons within the city boundaries. Major Dinwiddie paid his fine, and Steve and I compensated him for the moose meat at one dollar per pound, including the bones. That's what he had paid for it. Meat prices were expensive that year.

I'm only describing what I witnessed firsthand. And now I'll share something else with you. I watched Spot fall through a hole in the ice. The ice was three and a half feet thick, yet the current pulled him under like he was nothing more than a piece of straw. Three hundred yards downstream was the large water hole that the hospital used. Spot emerged from the hospital water hole, shook off the water, chewed out the ice that had formed between his toes, ran up the riverbank, and beat up a large Newfoundland dog that belonged to the Gold Commissioner.

In the fall of 1898, Steve and I poled up the Yukon on the last water, heading for Stewart River. We brought the dogs with us, all except Spot. We decided we'd been feeding him long enough. He'd cost us more time and trouble and money and food than we'd gotten by selling him on the Chilcoot—especially food. So Steve and I tied him up in the cabin and took off with our gear. We made camp that night at the mouth of Indian River, and Steve and I were pretty pleased with ourselves for having ditched him. Steve was a funny guy, and I was just sitting up in the blankets and laughing when chaos hit our camp. The way that Spot tore into those dogs and gave them a beating was terrifying. Now how did he break free? That's anyone's guess. I don't have any explanation. And how did he get across the Klondike River? That's another mystery. And besides, how did he know we had gone up the Yukon? You see, we went by water, and he couldn't pick up our scent. Steve and I started to get superstitious about that dog. He got on our nerves, too; and, between you and me, we were just a little bit afraid of him.

The freeze-up arrived while we were at the mouth of Henderson Creek, and we traded him away for two sacks of flour to a group that was heading up White River to search for copper. That entire group disappeared completely. No trace, sign, or remnant of the men, dogs, sleds, or anything else was ever discovered. They vanished without a trace. It became one of the unsolved mysteries of the region. Steve and I continued our journey up the Stewart, and six weeks later that dog Spot dragged himself into our camp. He was nothing but skin and bones, barely able to move forward, but somehow he made it there. What I want to understand is how he knew we were up the Stewart. We could have traveled to countless other locations. How did he figure it out? You explain that to me, and I'll explain it to you.

No way we were losing him. At the Mayo River, he got into a fight with an Indian's dog. The man who owned the dog swung an axe at Spot, missed him completely, and ended up killing his own dog instead. People talk about magic and deflecting bullets—but I think it's a lot harder to make someone miss with an axe when there's a strong man swinging it. And I witnessed this with my own eyes. That man had no intention of killing his own dog. You'd have to prove it to me otherwise.

I told you about Spot breaking into our meat supply. It nearly killed us. There wasn't any more meat to be hunted, and meat was all we had to survive on. The moose had traveled back several hundred miles and the Indians went with them. There we were. Spring was coming, and we had to wait for the river to thaw. We got pretty skinny before we decided to eat the dogs, and we decided to eat Spot first. Do you know what that dog did? He ran away. Now how did he know we had made up our minds to eat him? We stayed up nights waiting for him, but he never came back, and we ate the other dogs. We ate the entire team.

And now for what happened next. You know what it's like when a massive river breaks up and several billion tons of ice flow downstream, jamming together and churning and crushing everything in their path. Right in the middle of all that chaos, when the Stewart River broke up with thundering and roaring sounds, we spotted Spot out there in the center of it all. He'd gotten trapped while trying to cross somewhere upstream. Steve and I shouted and yelled and ran back and forth along the riverbank, throwing our hats up in the air. Sometimes we'd pause and embrace each other, we were so excited, because we could see that this was the end for Spot. He didn't stand even the slightest chance of surviving. He had absolutely no chance whatsoever. After the ice flow passed, we climbed into a canoe and paddled downstream to the Yukon River, and then down the Yukon to Dawson, taking time to rest and eat for a week at the cabins located at Henderson Creek's mouth. And as we approached the shore at Dawson, there was that same Spot, sitting there waiting for us, his ears standing alert, his tail wagging enthusiastically, his mouth appearing to smile, giving us a warm welcome. So how did he manage to escape from that ice? How did he know we were heading to Dawson, arriving at that exact hour and minute, to be sitting there on the riverbank waiting for us?

The more I think about that Spot, the more convinced I become that there are things in this world that go beyond science. That Spot cannot be explained on any scientific grounds. It's psychic phenomena, or mysticism, or something along those lines, I suppose, with a lot of Theosophy mixed in. The Klondike is a good country. I might have still been there, and become a millionaire, if it hadn't been for Spot. He got on my nerves. I put up with him for two years altogether, and then I guess my stamina gave out. It was the summer of 1899 when I left. I didn't say anything to Steve. I just snuck away. But I handled it properly. I wrote Steve a note, and included a package of "rough-on-rats," telling him what to do with it. I was worn down to skin and bone by that Spot, and I was so nervous that I'd jump and look around when there wasn't anybody within shouting distance. But it was amazing how quickly I recovered once I got rid of him. I gained back twenty pounds before I reached San Francisco, and by the time I'd taken the ferry across to Oakland I was my old self again, so much so that even my wife looked in vain for any change in me.

Steve wrote to me once, and his letter seemed annoyed. He was pretty upset because I had left him with Spot. He also mentioned that he had used the "rough-on-rats" exactly as instructed, but it hadn't worked at all. A whole year passed. I was back at the office and doing well in every way—I was even putting on some weight. Then Steve showed up. He didn't come to see me. I saw his name on the passenger list and wondered why he hadn't contacted me. But I didn't have to wonder for long. I woke up one morning to find Spot chained to my gate-post, terrorizing the milkman. I found out that Steve had headed north to Seattle that very same morning. I stopped gaining weight after that. My wife made me buy Spot a collar and tag, and within an hour he showed his appreciation by killing her beloved Persian cat. There's no way to get rid of that Spot. He'll stay with me until I die, because he'll never die. My appetite hasn't been the same since he arrived, and my wife says I'm looking thin and sickly. Last night Spot broke into Mr. Harvey's chicken coop (Harvey lives next door) and killed nineteen of his prize chickens. I'm going to have to pay for them. My neighbors on the other side got into an argument with my wife and then moved away. Spot caused that too. And that's why I'm so disappointed in Stephen Mackaye. I had no idea he could be such a cruel person.

THE END

Thank You For Reading

You've Just Read a Piece of the Greatest Library Ever Rebuilt

Thank you for reading.

This book is one of thousands we're restoring, reimagining, and translating as part of the **Modern Library of Alexandria** — a global movement to preserve and share humanity's most important ideas.

What was once lost to fire and time is now rising again — not just as memory, but as living, breathing knowledge, freely accessible to all.

What You Can Do Next:

* **Keep Reading.**

  Discover more legendary works — in beautiful print, audiobook, or digital form — at LibraryofAlexandria.com.

* **Build Your Own Library.**

  Every title is available as a paperback, hardcover, or collectible boxset — at true printing cost. Craft a personal library worthy of display.

* **Spread the Light.**

  Share this book. Tell others about the movement. Help us translate every timeless work into every language, so no reader is ever left behind.

By finishing this book, you've already taken part in something extraordinary.

Join us at LibraryofAlexandria.com

Together, we're rebuilding the greatest library the world has ever known.

With appreciation,

The Modern Library of Alexandria Team

Visit:
www.libraryofalexandria.com
Or scan the code below: